Inside the Sun and Moon

A poetry collection

linktr.ee/theapatheticpotato

Copyright © 2023 Hazel Allen

All rights reserved.

Images for book covers
designed on Canva.

*To everyone who
has supported my writing.*

Thank you.

Moonlit Queen

Are you like the sun as it arises?
Bright and warm, so full of splendor?
Your beauty, so gallant, my apprises;
To hold that heat, I'd be your contender.

Are you confident like the moon at night?
So mystifying, yet calm and serene?
You're unafraid to give us your light,
Confident and alluring; the Moonlit Queen.

You live among stories and folktales,
And only so many will seek your grace.
But truth is, you live among the golden trails:
The stars we see at night, adrift inside space.

If only I could reach you way out there,
But I'm your servant still, just elsewhere.

Lovers in the Vineyard

In the distance, from afar

I watch two pairs of hands

Holding each other and dancing

In the middle of a vineyard

The sun shining gently above

As they brush past vines of

Purple grapes, soft and tender

Her summer red dress

And their spring green tie

The glistening in her eyes

And their admiration shown

Through a pair of steadily

Flustering rosy red cheeks

The wind is bristling and the

Sun sets in its solemn nature

The two pause to watch as

The fiery orb of orange and red

Falls towards the horizon;

Heading to enlighten the

Other side of their fair planet

And as she studies the star

With all her excitement and wonder

They take her hand in theirs

Gentling caressing it with their thumb

And humming softly as the

Sky fades from warmth into the

Deeper blues and purples of the night

Two bodies so in touch together
In a beautiful farmstead with love
And peace within themselves
And in conjunction with each other
Enough to make me pause
To marvel at the thought of it

Enough to make me ponder
Whether one day I too will feel
The passion that they share
For each other in this field
Out in the country among those
Wine grapes or amidst the
City where some choose to
Never rest and be at home

A ghost with love on its mind.

I am on my way, under the moonlight,
Wandering through the empty streets-
Drifting quietly as if I were a specter
With an unfinished task between we;
If the moment arose to confess it,
I would finally proclaim my love to you.
But otherwise, I would let myself
Wander like the lost souls stuck deep
Within the growing fields of asphodel.
Unable to resonate with the confidence
I had admired from you so deeply-
But alas, perhaps one day I will drift
With everything I need in myself;
The tone and the swoon, to woo you forever.

A Beautiful Light

It's incredible, the light you emit–
Like a shooting star streaking across
The ever-darkening sky.

I wish I could beam with yellow,
Like you; you're a startling array of
Deeply entrenched sunlight.

You are like a beautiful constellation,
Resting in the atmosphere, just barely
Enough to be seen from the earth.

And I wonder if you'd like to dance,
Not like the sun and the moon in orbit,
But like two sea otters swimming close.

Then after we could snuggle
And share a sea urchin together, just
Before your light swallows me whole.

And I am then interwoven with
Every ounce of who you inspire
Me to be; a beautiful light, just like you.

Sun Story

You caught me in a smile,

Picking strawberries from the field.

Hazes of sun woven in

The seeds of the crops sown.

You're my happy summer smile,

The warmth deep in my blush,

Solis.

Sunlight

The sun emits beams
Shooting through your window
Giving off rays of light

Bringing waves of warmth
Perhaps when the world feels
Too cold, too bitter

But in time, its season
Becomes too old and I'm left
Feeling sick of it

Maybe I don't want to see yellow

Because I know only blue

Follows a setting sun

Cold, dark, loneliness only

Exempt by the dim light

Of a moon who remains

Alone, not by necessity but

Because it wants to be

Be kind to yourself

Be kind to yourself
For you will climb mountains
Before you love yourself.

Look into the mirror
And give yourself a compliment
For you're here all yourself.

I know you're barely clinging
Onto the image you've created,
Trying to fix who you are.

I know you just want to feel

Like you matter at all and

I'm here to say that you do.

So be kind to yourself because

You're a big part of this world,

And it still wants you here.

So be kind to yourself because

You're a light in the darkness-

A beacon of everything that I

Have longed to be.

The chains may be weighing
On your neck and shoulders,
But they're only inside.

And though it is difficult,
You will eventually break free
And feel that burden lifted.

You will find that hand to hold
And a soft voice affirming all
Of your needs and desires.

And you will find that one
To hold you and let you know
That you shine just like the sun.

Be kind to yourself
Because you're destined
For greatness.

Be kind to yourself
Because you are the current
That pushes this boat.

You are beautiful.
You are wonderful.
And you are amazing
Just the way you are.

Are you still here?

It is when night comes, that I sit alone here,

Thinking about how I'm lost now that you're gone;

Wishing I could just hide myself, to simply disappear.

The darkness outside I no longer fear,

And though friends keep me from being withdrawn-

It is when night comes, that I sit alone here,

Could I ask you if you're still near,

Or am I stuck in my head about what went on,

Wishing I could just hide myself, to simply disappear?

It's as if the sky had shed more than a single tear,

And though a downcast won't leave me left undergone

It is when night comes, that I sit alone here,

The grass will continue to grow, not sorely severe,

But just enough to keep me from dastardly thinking on,

Wishing I could just hide myself, to simply disappear.

I know my friend, your death is not the final frontier,

And though time will pass and I will move on,

It is when night comes, that I sit alone here,

Wishing I could just hide myself, to simply, disappear.

Citrus Tree

A citrus tree sits alone

In the middle of a barren field,

Under a light blue sky.

And as the birds come to

Accept its sweet offerings,

It smiles softly to itself.

For the life around has

Given it purpose in return

For its humble fruit.

So there it can rest knowing

That though it may be alone,

It still has the birds to call its own.

Daydream Butterfly

Peace, solidarity.
They come to mind.
Lo-fi beats and a
Calming train ride.

The fields outside are beautiful.
Parks shine with streams
Of magical waters from around.
The sun sets, rather, gently.

There is something natural,
About being here this evening.
Train tracks, rugged empathy.
Soaring by, given Nature's
Therapy.

Happiness, fulfillment.

This comes to mind

Can I stay here forever?

Or at least, some days?

Peace, solidarity.

They rest deep inside.

Lo-fi beats and a

Calming ride, *home.*

About the Author

Hazel Allen is an avid queer reader and writer based in Portland, Oregon. They first started writing in their Sophomore year of highschool, posting their poems over on Wattpad. Since then, they have branched out into other forms of writing too, like short stories, and some bigger projects.

When they're not writing, they enjoy playing videogames, going outside and being in nature, or learning a new hobby. They also like to collect various things, such as rubber duckies, pokemon cards, and puzzles.

You can check out more of their work over at:
linktr.ee/theapatheticpotato or
theapatheticpotato.wixsite.com